MEGA-COOL
MEGAFAUNA
Creatures of Ancient Seas
Anastasia Suen

Before Reading: *Building Background Knowledge and Vocabulary*

Building background knowledge can help children process new information and build upon what they already know. Before reading a book, it is important to tap into what children already know about the topic. This will help them develop their vocabulary and increase their reading comprehension.

Questions and Activities to Build Background Knowledge:

1. Look at the front cover of the book and read the title. What do you think this book will be about?
2. What do you already know about this topic?
3. Take a book walk and skim the pages. Look at the table of contents, photographs, captions, and bold words. Did these text features give you any information or predictions about what you will read in this book?

Vocabulary: *Vocabulary Is Key to Reading Comprehension*

Use the following directions to prompt a conversation about each word.

- Read the vocabulary words.
- What comes to mind when you see each word?
- What do you think each word means?

Vocabulary Words:
- carnivores
- cephalopods
- conical
- crustaceans
- extinction
- fossils
- herbivores
- megafauna
- omnivores
- organisms

During Reading: *Reading for Meaning and Understanding*

To achieve deep comprehension of a book, children are encouraged to use close reading strategies. During reading, it is important to have children stop and make connections. These connections result in deeper analysis and understanding of a book.

 Close Reading a Text

During reading, have children stop and talk about the following:

- Any confusing parts
- Any unknown words
- Text to text, text to self, text to world connections
- The main idea in each chapter or heading

Encourage children to use context clues to determine the meaning of any unknown words. These strategies will help children learn to analyze the text more thoroughly as they read.

When you are finished reading this book, turn to the next-to-last page for **Text-Dependent Questions** and an **Extension Activity**.

Table of Contents

The Ancient Seas

How do we know what lived in the sea long ago? **Fossils**! Ancient bones, shells, and other parts of living things washed up on seashores, where people found them. Finding fossils led people such as Mary Anning to discover **megafauna**.

The rocks on this beach in Lyme Regis, England, sometimes have fossils in them.

When she was 12, her brother Joseph found a skull on the beach near their home in England. What could it be? Mary wanted to know, so she spent months digging up sand around the bones to see the entire creature. In total, it was 17 feet (5.2 meters) long!

A Sea Monster?

Some people said that Mary had found a sea monster, but scientists thought Mary had found the skeleton of a crocodile. They argued about what it was for years before naming it Ichthyosaurus, *which means "fish lizard."*

This* Ichthyosaurus *skeleton has been preserved for millions of years.

Giant, unusual life forms filled the seas long before humans ever lived.

Ancient seas were filled with megafauna. What was it like to live in the sea long ago? Scientists say that 299 million to 273 million years ago, there was only one continent and one giant ocean. They named this land Pangaea and called the ocean around it Panthalassa.

As time passed, Pangaea slowly broke apart, and new continents formed. The continents and the oceans around them were given new names.

Pangaea

Asia

Europe

North
America

Africa

South
America

Panthalassa

Antarctica

Australia

From One Ocean to Five

*The Pacific Ocean, the Atlan
Ocean, the Arctic Ocean, and
Indian Ocean are the oldest
oceans. In 2000, the Souther
Ocean (circling Antarctica) w
named by the International
Hydrographic Organization.*

The World Today

Arctic Ocean

North
America

Europe

Asia

Atlantic
Ocean

Africa

South
America

Pacific
Ocean

Indian
Ocean

Australia

Southern Ocean

Antarctica

Did you know that oceans cover about 70 percent of the Earth's surface? That gave sea creatures a lot of room to grow! What did they eat to become mega-sized?

Just like people, ancient sea creatures ate different things. Some were **herbivores** and only ate plants. Some were **carnivores** and only ate meat. Some were **omnivores** and ate everything.

The earliest seas contained only tiny **organisms**. Over time, living things were able to grow larger and more complex. Eventually, megafauna developed. Ancient sea creatures started snacking in the seas during the Mesozoic Era. You live in the Quaternary Period of the Cenozoic Era.

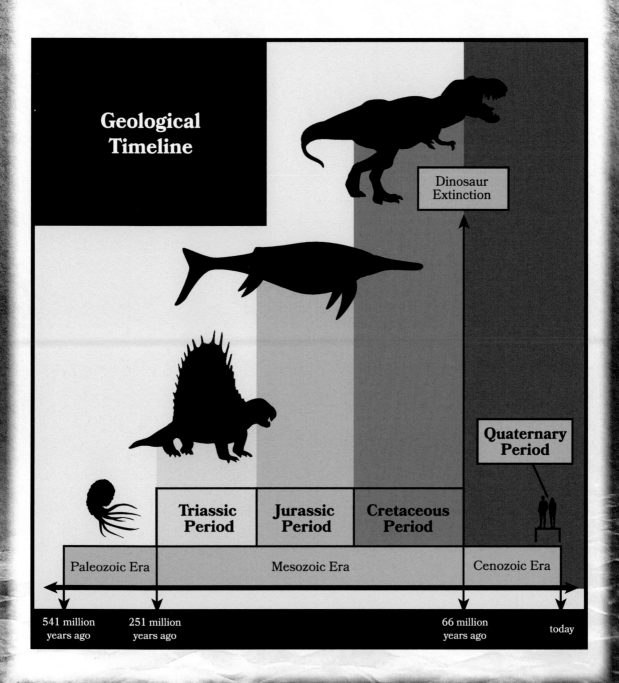

Geological Timeline

Dinosaur Extinction

Quaternary Period

	Triassic Period	Jurassic Period	Cretaceous Period	
Paleozoic Era		Mesozoic Era		Cenozoic Era

| 541 million years ago | 251 million years ago | | 66 million years ago | today |

Not all cows live on land. Sea cows lived in shallow waters along the coast during the Ice Age. That was 2.6 million to 11,700 years ago!

The skeleton of the extinct Steller's sea cow is on display at the Museum of Nature of the Kharkiv National University.

In 1741, sailors discovered a herd of sea cows living in the Arctic waters. They named them after the scientist on their ship, Georg Steller. These 20,000-pound (9,072-kilogram) mammals grew up to 30 feet (nine meters) long by eating seagrass and seaweed. The meat of one Steller's sea cow could feed the ship's crew for a month. Less than 30 years later, people had hunted them into **extinction**.

Most of the megafauna in the ancient seas were carnivores. Big creatures ate small creatures—and grew even bigger!

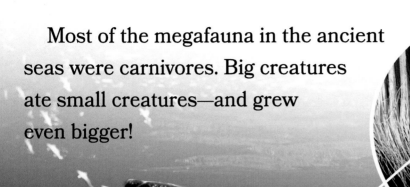

baleen plates

A Big Gulp

To eat, a blue whale takes a big gulp of water, closes its mouth, and pushes the water out with its tongue. As water flows out through its baleen plates, thousands of tiny animals called krill are trapped inside. Gulp!

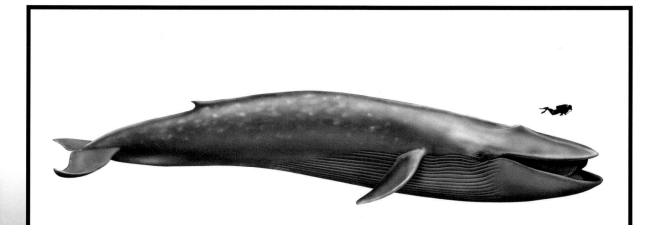

Humans are tiny in comparison to a blue whale.

The biggest ancient sea creature is still alive today. Blue whales have been around for 36 million years. They weren't always mega-sized, though. During the Ice Age, not much food was available for blue whales. The ones that survived were the ones who grew larger. At 90 feet (27 meters), a blue whale is as long as two school buses. This giant can weigh 300,000 pounds (136,078 kilograms). Its tongue weighs as much as an elephant!

Mary Anning found the first ichthyosaur, a swimming reptile, in 1821. At 17 feet (5.2 meters) long, it was the size of a pickup truck. In 2011, a different kind of ichthyosaur made the record books. *Shastasaurus* was 69 feet (21 meters) long. It was five pickup trucks long!

octopus

squid

cuttlefish

Most ichthyosaurs had long snouts with small, **conical** teeth. They used to catch fish and **cephalopods** such as octopus, squid, cuttlefish, and shellfish called ammonites. But *Shastasaurus* slurped up little cephalopods and swallowed them whole!

Long-necked plesiosaurs also swam in the sea. They looked like a turtle *and* a snake! The one with the longest neck was an *Elasmosaurus*. It used its long neck to catch fish. Scientists found a mega-sized one in Antarctica that took four trips to dig out of the rock. Why? It was almost 40 feet (12 meters) long and weighed about 30,000 pounds (13,607 kilograms).

The Loch Ness Monster

Some people said that this Antarctic plesiosaur proved that the Loch Ness Monster was real. The Loch Ness lake formed 10,000 years ago, and plesiosaurs have been extinct for more than 65 million years.

The first mosasaur was discovered in the state of Kansas, United States, in 1868 during the "Bone Wars." Two old friends, Othniel C. Marsh and Edward Drinker Cope, and their team of scientists competed to name the most fossils. Their teams looked in the same places and often gave the same bones different names!

Kansas is far from any sea or ocean. So why look there for ancient sea life? In the late Cretaceous period, the middle of North America was underwater. Mosasaurs swam in a large body of water called the Western Interior Seaway.

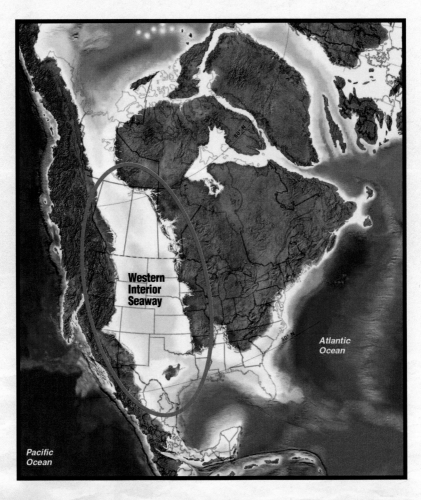

More than Meets the Eye

From the front, Tylosaurus looked small, but it was 45 feet (17 meters) long! It used its long tail to swim and hunt turtles, fish, seabirds, octopus, squid, plesiosaurs, ammonites—and other mosasaurs.

Chomp! The largest shark tooth in the world is a megalodon tooth. These sharp, jagged teeth could grow to more than seven inches long measured at an angle. It's no wonder why this animal's name means "big tooth." A four-million-year-old megalodon found in Peru had 222 teeth in its huge jaws. Nothing in the water was safe from this massive shark. After growing up to 59 feet (18 meters) long, these 100,000-pound (45,359 kilogram) sharks even ate whales.

Dragon Tongues!

People have found megalodon teeth for thousands of years. The Romans said they fell from the sky. Until 1667, some people thought they had found dragon tongues that turned into stones!

A megalodon tooth (left) is huge compared to a modern shark's tooth (right).

In 2008, scientists found a whale skull that was 10 feet (three meters) long. They estimated that it was around the same size as a megalodon: 50 feet (15 meters) long and 100,000 pounds (45,359 kilograms). *Livyatan's* modern relatives only have small teeth in their bottom jaw. *Livyatan* had teeth in both jaws that were 12 inches (30 centimeters) long and four inches (10 centimeters) wide. It could eat any animal it wanted, including other whales.

Pieces of backbone from Livyatan were preserved in this chunk of rock.

Mega Numbers

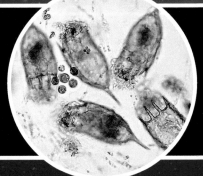

The biggest fish in the world ate copepods—tiny **crustaceans** *floating in the water. Copepods in water everywhere, even today. Scientists have found more than 11,500 kinds of copepods.*

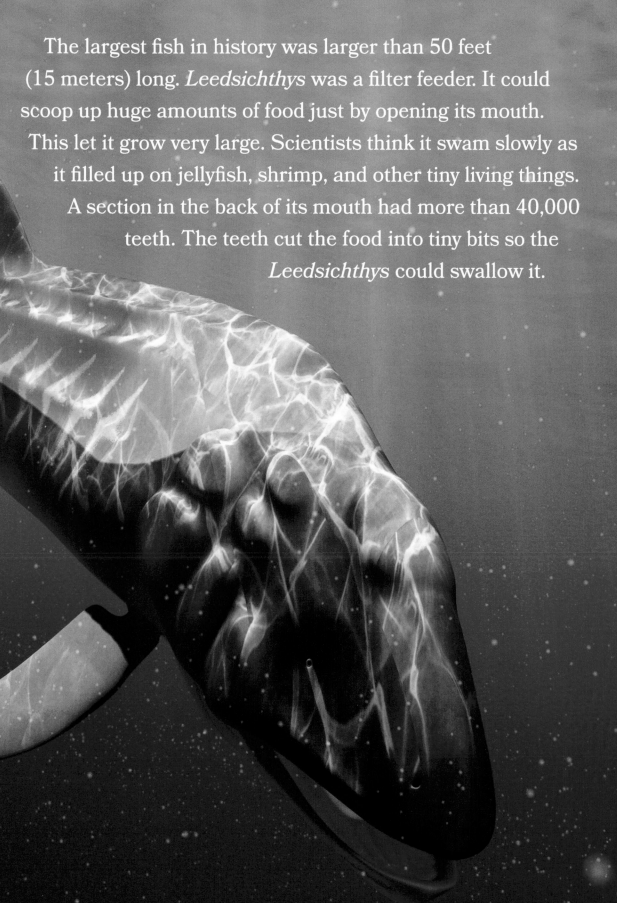

The largest fish in history was larger than 50 feet (15 meters) long. *Leedsichthys* was a filter feeder. It could scoop up huge amounts of food just by opening its mouth. This let it grow very large. Scientists think it swam slowly as it filled up on jellyfish, shrimp, and other tiny living things. A section in the back of its mouth had more than 40,000 teeth. The teeth cut the food into tiny bits so the *Leedsichthys* could swallow it.

Swimming near the surface of the water, the ancient sea turtle *Archelon* ate both fish and plants. Even ammonites were on the menu. *Archelon*'s sharp beak could break shells! Fossils from this Cretaceous-period sea turtle were found in the state of South Dakota. It was 16 feet (4.8 meters) from nose to tail and 13 feet wide (four meters) from flipper to flipper. Scientists think it weighed about 4,500 pounds (2,200 kilograms).

A Long Life

The largest and most complete Archelon *fossil ever found is displayed in the Vienna Museum of Natural History. Scientists think this* Archelon *was 100 years old when it died while hibernating in the mud.*

Models such as this one can help people understand how Archelon **ate and moved.**

Still Searching

People find new scientific information every day. No one knows what will be discovered next. Every new fossil helps scientists learn more. What they find helps them look at the fossils they already have in new ways. Will you be the one who makes the next big discovery?

Big, Bigger, Biggest

None of the ancient sea creatures shown here were weighed or measured on a scale when they were alive. Scientists made their best guess about the creatures' size based on fossils.

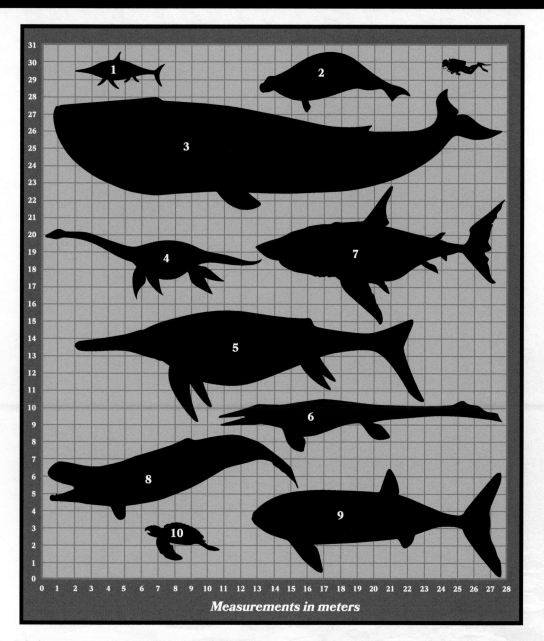

Measurements in meters

1. *Ichthyosaurus* 17 feet (5.2 meters) long
2. Steller's sea cow 30 feet (nine meters) long
3. blue whale 90 feet (27 meters) long
4. *Elasmosaurus* 40 feet (12 meters) long
5. *Shastasaurus* 69 feet (21 meters) long
6. *Tylosaurus* 45 feet (17 meters) long
7. megalodon 50 feet (15 meters) long
8. *Livyatan* 50 feet (15 meters) long
9. *Leedsichthys* 50 feet (15 meters) long
10. *Archelon* 16 feet (4.8 meters) long

Glossary

carnivores (KAHR-nuh-vorz): animals that eat only other animals

cephalopods (SEF-uh-luh-pods): mollusks with tentacles attached to the head, including the cuttlefish, squid, and octopus

conical (KON-ik-uhl): shaped like a cone with a pointed top and sides that form a circle at the bottom

crustaceans (kruh-STEY-shuns): animals with a hard body covering that live in the water, including lobsters, shrimp, crabs, and barnacles

extinction (ik-STINGK-shuhn): when something such as a plant or animal species has died out completely

fossils (FOS-uh-ls): remains, impressions, or traces of a living thing from a former geologic age, such as a skeleton or footprint

herbivores (HUR-buh-vorz): animals that eat only plants

megafauna (MEG-uh-faw-nuh): large or giant animals

omnivores (AHM-nuh-vorz): animals that eat both plants and other animals

organisms (AWR-guh-niz-uhms): life forms such as animals or plants

Index

Text-Dependent Questions

1. Where did Mary Anning find an ancient sea creature?

2. What were the "Bone Wars"?

3. How did ancient whales grow so large?

4. Why are there sea creature fossils in Kansas?

5. Why do you think most of the ancient sea megafauna were carnivores?

Extension Activity

Use air-dry clay to make your own ancient sea creature. Look for images of an ancient sea creature to use as a model. Then decide if you want to make a fossil or a 3-D image of the ancient sea creature while it was still alive. Let the clay dry for 72 hours.

About the Author

Anastasia Suen is the author of more than 350 books for children, teens, and adults. Although she has collected seashells from beaches around the world, she hasn't found an ancient sea fossil yet. She lives near the sea in Northern California, where whales and sharks swim as they migrate each year.

www.rourkeeducationalmedia.com

PHOTO CREDITS: cover: Shutterstock; page 3: Shutterstock; page 4: GettyImages / urbancow / René Mansi; page 5: GettyImages / Joaquin Corbalan; page 6: GettyImages / dottedhippo; pages 7-9: Shutterstock; page 10: Reprinted with permission from Encyclopædia Britannica, © 2010 by Encyclopædia Britannica, Inc.; page 11: Yacheslav Madiyevskyy / ZUMA Press / Newscom; page 12: GettyImages / bbevren (inset) / Francois Gohier / Oceans Image / Photoshot / Newscom (inset) / GettyImages / Leamus; page 13: Reprinted with permission from Encyclopædia Britannica, © 2010 by Encyclopædia Britannica, Inc.; pages 14-15: Shutterstock; page 15: (insets) Shutterstock / Barry Brown / DanitaDelimont. com Danita Delimont Photography / Newscom; pages 16-17: GettyImages / Daniel Eskridge; page 17: gettyimages / © Matt84; page 18: Staff / MCT / Newscom; pages 19-21: Shutterstock; page 21: (inset) Shutterstock; page 22: World History Archive / Newscom; page 23: Lex van Groningen / Buiten-beeld / Minden Pictures / Newscom; page 24: (inset) Shutterstock; pages 24-25: SCIEPRO / SCIENCE PHOTO LIBRARY / Science Photo Library / Newscom; page 26: Shutterstock; page 27: (inset) Shutterstock / (inset) Richard Graulich / ZUMA Press / Newscom; page 28: GettyImages

Edited by: Tracie Santos
Cover and interior design by: Lynne Schwaner

Library of Congress PCN Data

Creatures of Ancient Seas / Anastasia Suen
(Mega-Cool Megafauna)
ISBN 978-1-73164-349-0 (hard cover)(alk. paper)
ISBN 978-1-73164-313-1 (soft cover)
ISBN 978-1-73164-381-0 (e-Book)
ISBN 978-1-73164-413-8 (ePub)
Library of Congress Control Number: 2020945097

Rourke Educational Media
Printed in the United States of America
02-1072311937